PARDON MY HEART

PARDON MY HEART

POEMS

MARCUS JACKSON

TRIQUARTERLY BOOKS / NORTHWESTERN UNIVERSITY PRESS

EVANSTON, ILLINOIS

TriQuarterly Books
Northwestern University Press
www.nupress.northwestern.edu

Printed in the United States of America

10   9   8   7   6   5   4   3   2   1

Library of Congress Cataloging-in-Publication Data
Names: Jackson, Marcus, 1981– author.
Title: Pardon my heart : poems / Marcus Jackson.
Description: Evanston, Illinois : TriQuarterly Books/Northwestern University
    Press, 2018.
Identifiers: LCCN 2017049451| ISBN 9780810136915 (pbk. : alk. paper) |
    ISBN 9780810136922 (ebook)
Subjects: LCSH: African Americans—Social life and customs—Poetry. |
    LCGFT: Love poetry.
Classification: LCC PS3610.A35427 P37 2018 | DDC 811/.6—dc23
LC record available at https://lccn.loc.gov/2017049451

Your pulse must not say
What must not be said.

—GWENDOLYN BROOKS

CONTENTS

PART ONE

PART TWO

PART THREE

PART FOUR

PART ONE

PART ONE

PARDON MY HEART

Pardon my heart if it ruins your party.
It's a large, American heart and has had

a good deal to drink. It's a pretty bad
dancer—too much feeling, too little technique.

It may sing some godless hymns, about ousting
armies of loneliness, about marching

victorious to wives and towns beneath
a heart-colored dusk. Pardon my heart

if it closes its eyes for hours,
whispering *rapture* over and over.

Pardon my heart if it laughs too loudly,
or if it tells many of its stories

too ardently. Pardon my heart if it rests
an arm across you or your friends' shoulders—

touch allows my heart to trust that it's not
imagining your company's loveliness.

Pardon my heart if you have to kick it out.
After you've muzzled the music and brightened

the lights to tidy, my heart will ignore
and keep doing its little two-step, aglow

in the middle of the room, never
happier to have nowhere else to go.

PARADISE SKATE

Friday nights, we waited in a loud line
for the door's push bars to unchain,
for the admission lady wearing a stiff wig
to collect the two-dollar cover.
Beforehand, we stood at murky mirrors,
girls penciling eyeliner or ironing
greased kinks, boys honing poses
or spraying counterfeit cologne.
Above shelves of beige skates for rent,
the wall wore a mural of a tropical beach,
parrots squawking in the painted trees.
Dimness veiled the scarred parquet, a DJ
clawing songs as we sang and rapped along.
Two lots west, the Powertrain Plant kindled
engines and differentials to blind life.
In the suburbs, our counterparts bladed
on ice, their cheeks opening into rosiness.
We shimmied on small, oiled wheels,
until sweat glazed our faces, until motion
swept the debris from our beings,
until big bulbs in the rafters thundered
and we winced in the godly watts,
godly for not allowing us to live
any longer on delight's tiny island.

BASS

We saved up for old
   Regals or Fleetwoods, pulled
the spares from their trunks,
   making way for pairs

of subwoofers, amplifiers
   with enough wattage
to shock polar bears,
   and we drove slow, so our

music's bass would shake
   cars in the next lane,
shake the asphalt
   when traffic choked, shake

the comely blades
   of yards whose owners might
write our plate numbers, shake
   our transmissions from slipping,

shake our origins'
   implications, shake the stars
to falling salt, shake the moon
   to a quivering dish, and shake

by night's end the precarious
   straightness from the hair
of our dates, who
   sometimes sang.

IF ONLY

If only I could sing like Marvin,
in a blue room, while the rain sounds
like raw rice spilling.
If only I could sing like an overweight
bank account. If only I could sing
as southern as Muddy, as electrically
as Jimi. If only I could sing
in the subway, with train brakes
jumping in as my metal section.
If only a needle drank my cries
from looping grooves in black wax.
If only I could sing risen
the conjoined wishbones written
on sheet music. If only I could sing
fields onward toward burgeoning,
sing stubborn kings into listening,
sing babies in pain to sleep.
If only my voice were swallows
of ripe wine. If only my voice could be
a handsome hand on night's thigh.

EVEN WHEN SPILLING

I've got to do something with all this longing
I think, listening to the interstate
sound so purposeful as I walk the overpass
with a flask, the dusk heavy as a held tongue.
During the day, amplifications
of my mistakes—long ago and recent—
kept deafening the edges of me.
Of course, so many greater disturbances
than my own, so many magnified atoms
of unease are spreading through larger
more important elsewheres.
But the U.S. is the realm of the self,
so I'm telling you of mine—a self which,
even when spilling, is such a thirsty thing.

TO THE LOVE GODS

Thanks for those first dearests
who left us for flashier suitors.
Thanks for guiding us away
from sleeping with the misleading people
who seemed fine at the time: the woman
who ended up the queen in a monarchy
of rescued cats; the man who killed
a clerk during a robbery. Thanks again
for the condoms that didn't break,
for Mrs. Moore using a cucumber
in health class to so clearly demonstrate
how to put a Trojan on.
Thanks for the morning-after pill,
for abortion, for the absolution in both
escape and regret. Thanks for all
the solitude, all the nights our rooms
were the monologues of stones.
Thanks for all the quarrels, the furious
mouths and unbelievable words.
Thanks for your permission to mend,
for prescribing time and somber songs
as balms. And thanks of course
for our hearts, those redundant drums,
ushering us through the darkness that lives
between the burning kingdoms of our loves.

WHEN IN LOVE

You're a drooling fool—you've got a mouth
full of diamonds, and you're smiling.
Your body is a key, tied
to a kite bitten by lightning.
Troubling memories have dug escapes
from the cellblocks of your brain.
You're a piece of luminous fruit
yet to be bruised.
You gasp the way waves at night crash,
and you moan like a full moon.
You're something extremely expensive
carried by a clumsy kid.
Spring, its worm-gorged birds and redbud trees,
can't even keep up with your jubilee.

WHEN OUT OF LOVE

You're a rowboat at the center
of a desert. You're tongueless
and all your words blur.
Your hands are blind birds.
Your mind is a long ride
on the wrong bus. Your sleep is
brief, and the smallest sounds are
rifle rounds cracking prairie air.
The police have your cheek
against their car hood and they're cuffing you.
The sun is the sourest fruit.
The stars are silver
dust at the bottom of a robbed strongbox.
The children playing in the alley scream
like dropped rucksacks full of glass.
You're a missing miner
and you dig so far the dark
holds you better than a mother.

CONVALESCENCE

The finest part of losing a fistfight
occurred the hour after, assuming
you had a girlfriend to go to. She'd sit you
on the bathroom counter, she'd cotton ball
Neosporin to your bashed brow, your split
cheek, your lip like a scrap left over
by a butcher. Her hands would weigh no more
than birch leaves; her exhales would sweep your ears
like wind through creek weeds. From a radio,
Mary J. Blige would be testifying.
Beneath the bulbs' glare, your knuckles would unbind,
your arms would dissolve, you'd close your eyes and be
some lost soldier wasp, healing the entire
night in the middle of a magnolia.

DOMINION OF MEN

In tenth grade, I knocked out someone
twice my age and weight—Larry, a veteran
with a wrecked knee, who begged my friend and me
to taste the spicy joint we blazed.

Larry could usually be seen on a lawn chair,
nodding between the brushstrokes of numbness
heroin painted in his veins.
We refused to share our smoke, and I made

a joke that spurred Larry to an anger
in which he called us niggers and began
swinging his metal cane. I threw a left-hand straight
that popped open Larry's cheek; he dropped

and bled heavily. For weeks, my buddies
spread tales of the triumph to everyone,
but the punch was luck, a thoughtless reaction
that found the unguarded head of an addict

who'd racked up enough petty wrongs
to earn a defeat from a skinny teen.
Larry has since gone completely to dirt,
his gravestone laid flat on the grass,

his name underscored by the chiseled words
SOLDIER, FATHER, BROTHER, SON.
I have a son now. I'll soon teach him the bit
of boxing I know, his fists harmless as balled dough.

Eventually, those fists could win him entry
into the strange dominion of men, where faces
grow grim during stories of love, and where faces
become bright throughout fables full of pain.

BEST MEN

to Jeff

Our voices used to be squeezed baby toys.
Eyeholes once gaped where the knees
of our jeans should've been. Our mothers wore
shiners, or spoke low from jail phones.
We notched honor rolls and scholarships.
A bullet shattered a windshield.
We found healthier cities and fell
into hospital rooms, prescriptions rattling
from cabinets. We touched the brass handles
of caskets. Fatherhood startled like a doorbell
middream. Fatherhood became a lake in waning
daylight. Now, we smoke a glass pipe on the patio,
the lighter flame lowering to the dope
like a torch to a naked brain. The night
insects begin their raspy symphony. We laugh
and settle into being men, into suits that fit
much truer once the lapels wilt, once
frayed thread hangs in a button's wake.

BABY BOY IN THE BACK ROOM

While a weekday party grew in the front
of a foul flat, you slept in a car seat
set upon a mattress that had no sheets.

You dreamed, and your young mother drank a quart
of malt, and she wouldn't smile until
a foam halo lay at the bottle's base.

Tunes with curses in the choruses boomed;
we teen boys roared and wore too much toughness.
Tramping back from the toilet, I saw you

and stepped close enough to hear
the ricocheting breeze of your breathing.
I thought of praying in that bedroom—

for your safety, or for the knobless door
to somehow slow down all the ugliness
building beyond. I chose only to crouch,

to kiss your head's tender top and return
to my pint of rank wine, my cigarette
left balancing on an upturned beer cap,

to one night in a great array of nights
when we hid our hurt and mistook the world
for an ordeal no father could make gentler.

PART TWO

EVASIVE ME

Of course there's a certificate, bleeding
carbon at the creases and impressions,

detailing my metrics and lineage the night
I entered the earthly air in a new hospital

built by the intricate partnership between
Rust Belt governance, capitalism,

and Christ, though I lie to people I like,
saying I was born in a garden so near

the sea that my mother—multilingual
and remarkably tall—rinsed me at the fringe

of the tide the morning after labor,
the horizon cloudless and birdless

while the sand whispered spells of protection,
depth and solemnity upon the pair of us,

and amidst this farce my dear listeners
don expressions of distrust or ire

as likely they should, faced with evasive
me, so wearied even before boyhood

by the truth that I've forever disallowed
my ears and my mouth any songs not made

from the water, dirt, wind, salt, and fire
of American manipulation.

LULLABY

to Jessica

Fighting with Mama, Dad shattered
a lamp, slammed the door, and headed
to the Ottawa Tavern. Mama took you
from your rickety crib, and we both sat
on her lap, as she smoked and hummed
in the unlit kitchen. Her Merit burned
on the glass ashtray, while Dad arrived at the pub
where the barmaid knew what he needed
before he spoke. What was Mama thinking,
her biceps bruised, her thin hair held back
by a doubled-up rubber band? Is there
a sure way to love a man the world won't
quit dealing trouble to? Why is the future
a fog-faced thing, whose teeth we can't see
before being bitten? That night, Mama simply
kept on humming—some song now lost
in the long line of exhausted songs—
and she swayed, until sleep's clean sheet
wrapped the brains of her babies.

OFF CAMERA

There remain some black-and-white photos
of my mother, snapped the August she left
for college. She's wearing a dark, long-sleeved

velvet dress, half an oval cut between
the shoulders, showing her clavicle.
The shoot ensued at the eastern skirts

of some woods, daylight leaking through the leaves.
In my favorite of these frames, she's looking
to her right, her face and eyes bearing a fierce

vulnerability. She was soon to begin
studying acting—at a school with touted
teachers, a city with buildings that took

steel bites of sky. In this shot, she peers
off camera as if, at sixteen, she already sees
the brutal plentitudes waiting to break her.

ASHTRAY

Filling with my mother's smolderings,
this tawny, six-sided, three-pound glass dish
has sat forty years at the table's center.
During lapses in labor or happiness,
Mother smoked Merit after Merit, her mind
a crowded parlor of plans, self-hate,
and urgent glimpses of encounters long past.
She split the skin atop my father's skull
once with this ashtray as he grabbed her.
Weekly, after she emptied and washed it, Friday's light
entered the drafty sash and upheld this ashtray
as the crown of one woman's quiet country.

ONE MORE TINY THING, 1985

Auntie kisses each dying catfish
before cleaning it. Lots of small, gold eggs fall
from the sliced gut of a female (a bullhead
Auntie caught herself). Her man labors home,
his work shirt blue-gray and machinery stained.
The two of them feast, drink tall cans of Miller
after saying a brief grace. Auntie stares
at his hands—blunt knuckles that will again
find her face during fights. That night, she dreams
of immense bass, carp, and trout that talk, that walk
on their tail fins, that give long, soggy hugs.
She wakes sweating, like all five times
fish have slipped into her sleep before,
certain one more tiny thing swims
the bothered waters within her.

ALTERNATE TAKE ON AUTUMN BEGINNING

I think of the bald practice field, of rehearsing
the playbook's blueprinted collisions,
of Coach Cunningham yelling into the caged
faces of us negroes. I think of Darnell,
our miraculous halfback, of his dad, the beautiful
blues drummer who burned their rent on a habit, I think
of the cheerleaders' humdrum rhymes, of game night
police eyeing the bleachers for fights,
of our mothers' drab jackets, pierced at the breast
by badges with our pictures, of the childless
teachers, looking in the mirror before pulling
themselves from their cars, of evening air spiked
with cedar needles, and of the burnished helmets
doubling our skulls so we could knock entirely
against the bolted doors of better births.

ARMOR

I stood in my underwear, the iron
clicking toward readiness. In yesterday's
slacks and wifebeater, my dad smoothed a leg
of my Lees on the timeworn pressing board.
Steam seeped between the denim and metal.
I dressed, the clothes warm as a second flesh,
my dad finding some duct tape, wrapping his hand
tacky side out. He patted lint from my chest
and shoulders; my kidneys echoed when he tapped
my back. I left for a day of first grade, light
sliding into our slim street like a blade
into a sheath, my dad ironing his own clothes
before once more entering a town
keen on cutting the wrong men down.

SWEETEST DAY

The student body government sold
dollar carnations in the cafeteria.
LaTrell, who many of our school's girls
knew of and loved, made a killing.
He bought no flowers for anyone, yet
ended the day with a jumbo bouquet,
a few admirers bold enough to give multiples.
He strutted the halls with a blinding smile,
the array of red petals and clipped stems
leaving a candied scent after he passed.
That Saturday, on a late-night street,
the metal handle of a high-caliber
pistol mangled his face when he refused
to yield his suede coat and Jordan 13s.
Before the leader of the robbery crew
began beating LaTrell, the guy turned
to his wordless accomplices and said,
Problem is, pretty niggas like this
gotta learn it hurt to be sweet.

CRACK COOK

On a triple beam Shaun stole from our school's
chemistry room, soda-cooked cocaine weighed
to exact grams. His mother waitressing
at a twilight diner, and his toddler
sister drowsing in her crib, Shaun chopped product
on the coffee table, cautious never
to waste a grain. He reveled especially
in the venture's finer details: his phone's
endless trembling; the feeding of folks
who woke to tongues as dry as baked slate;
the warmth of bill upon folded bill; the cops
in civilian sedans; and how, when his hand
opened, the streetlights were upturned spoons
dripping gleam onto each ivory crumb.

GOODALE PARK

A hunched man speaks Korean to the geese,
feeding them old bread at the pond brim
while much of the park late April
is a unified green breathing.
When the clusters of ducks bob
backward from submergence, their beaks look
lacquered, and they shimmy their wings
as if deflecting mortality.
A tall can of common beer in a paper sleeve
does now for me what the burgeoning season does
for the ducks; the yeasty froth and the slight sting
imbue some peace after a year of grieving
a brother who, in youth, screamed elatedly
when our mother, her eyes widened and softened
by codeine, first showed us how to draw
frenzies of the large, long-traveled birds
by tossing pieces of stale sourdough
onto the edge of the park's dark water.

FULL-TIME DRIVER

I took every hour they offered, delivering
lukewarm pizzas by means of an '86
LeSabre, the back tires almost bald.
Managers rarely yelled or wore me out
about moving too slow. When we blundered
orders, most customers understood.
My brother worked there too. He was beautiful.
I should've kissed him, one good forehead kiss
while such a gesture might've mattered.
Women, shoeless in their doorways, gave me
resigned smiles as they paid. Undergraduate
smokers proposed hits of their burning herb.
The richest part was when business
would ebb, and I'd coast the summer streets.
The air felt like a cool fruit. The engine block
churned a sure tune. The rearview caught
moments of low moons. Time was a tame lake
my hand skimmed from the front of a canoe.

WOMAN IN SECRET

My cousin eight and I five, he led me
to a gutted Econoline, propped
by cinders in a neighbor's side drive.
On the bare floor near a wheel well lay
a *Hustler*, peeled to its center pages.
Crouched in the smell of brake fluid
and leaked rain, my cousin pointed
to the woman (nude and spread-legged)
upon rumpled paper. *Dass Pussy*,
he whispered, the syllables rising
through the vast cabin. Not the breasts
or the ample insides of the thighs,
but the sleek, transfixing pink, her own
fingers pinning the flesh agape.
I hadn't yet lost my first tooth, couldn't
have contained the blatant light
of lust, yet I stared at that woman,
my senses blending and sharpening
as her furtive yearning breached me.

PART THREE

ONE TOUCH

There is so much flesh you'd like to touch
but don't—the incandescent neck
of a married coworker; the fine hands
of an acquaintance who enters your thoughts
while you lie alone in bed; the legs
of a lover you often touched, though ought
never touch again; the lips of striking
strangers in long lines or on buses.
One well-placed kiss, one measured occurrence
of contact is all your crux whispers for,
as if there are no larger desires
sure to extend throughout you, should you
be foolish or bold enough to reach toward
someone whose want is sharper than yours.

I DON'T DO THIS MUCH, BUT

I'm a sucker for the wondrously torn apart type,
and the stare you've been giving me is

quite the installment of radiant dismantlement.
I love this place, its overpoured bottom-shelf specials,

its stained ceiling tiles, and the way the daytime
street and people through the front window accent

my expedient bewilderment. For a second or so
I pondered not talking to you, leaving

the wavelengths of our respective singularities
to hum at different ends of the bar, and then my dead

mother's voice called out my cursed foolhood,
my faithlessness in distrusting the glaring likeliness

that you, over here—in an attire and posture
that must've accompanied you through miles

of disquiet, thrill, retreat, and dreaming—
swiftly drinking what I'm guessing is your

third gin gimlet, might become inclined to hear
a few more peculiar, fervent notes about

the outlandish soul my body hardly holds.

AGAIN

Again, cross the floorboards
with that walk of yours, the one that's more
psychology than body.
Again, tell me about before
we met, when you slept less
than the wind, when you rode
the same night bus until
the sky lost its opacity.
Have I told you yet
how I've been fine with dying
since the first morning I woke
to you peering out the window
drinking coffee in your underthings?
Sometimes when you leave
the room gapes,
and the sounds of the house harshen,
and your distance is
a bare dish gathering dust.
Again, let's take a plane somewhere
known for heavy rain spells.
We'll sit outside, barefoot
beneath an eave and not talk, watching
the falling water like an endless set
of instrument strings trembling.

SAME ROOM SOME NIGHTS

Of late, I've been getting along better
with my bartender than with my lover.
The rest of the regulars and I start early,
the morning light lying
on the tavern's urethaned wood, every
piece of dust vibrating slightly while lowering
or rising through the blinding air.
The words my lover and I used to use
are garments whose colors and fits have warped;
we have learned far too many
of one another's fragilities.
By the time we find the same room some nights,
our faces are answerless, our mouths like walls
to which vandals have taken hammers.

THE FORMER US

Remember when our bodies were novel,
when down to the particle were want and gloss?
Tonight, it takes a few drinks apiece and slight lies
for the former us to surface, for our mouths
to go buoyant, our eyes to wipe lambent.
For a song or two, we're our pre-procreation,
our pre-career, our pre-refinanced selves, walking
tipsy down an empty street, talking too loud,
groping each other, nearing your dark
one-windowed apartment, both of us wrongly sure
we won't do anything irreparable to each other.

SEPARATION

I'm watching a film full of our kind
of longing—the subtle, gradually mounting,
late evening kind of longing. The female lead's
main radiance is a mouth through with all
the common town's lukewarm words.
There's a man, too, in a brackish hat,
his jaw in one scene cutting the dusk
horizon as he turns to walk away.
The cinematography is a taken-apart
harmonica laid on dark felt,
making me finally see and praise the way
we left each other—disassembled
and motionless enough to be touched fully
by an intricate, tireless silence.

TRAVEL PLANS

All these nights, I've been telling you things,
mainly made-up things, aiming

for your wonder and empathy and lust,
and this has worked well enough, what

with you glimmering to others about my
victories and complexities, what with

us waking bare-fleshed while mornings
blared light through the shadeless panes.

But I'm talked out now, and the reach of requisite
is suddenly so fraught within you, your eyes

looking breakably at me, your parted mouth
the bay your former voice won't find, and I'm

leaving, maybe for a bar or a bus station,
cheap drinks alone or a slow, third-class ride

to another unremarkable town where
someone else's face will

in a half-second glance give me
the thrilling disinterest I need.

THE CROWN INN, WASHINGTON, D.C.

The woman working the night desk alone
has a miniature, bleeding rose
tattooed on her wrist, and her grin is as slight
as an incision. Ice machines center
every floor, droning and tremulous.
In room 414, a man sleeps on top
of the tucked sheets, his only company
the silenced TV—rerun comedies.
In the housekeeping closets wait boxes
of sparse soap bars, vacuums with lungs
of dust, and bottles that will sneeze
ammonia onto mirrors. In the morning
the curtains will recant, and the light will scream
like a dead king's gold falling into a sea.

DISREGARD

after Philip Levine

On a cold day cut by tart light
I stood on the loading dock and watched
a pair of teenaged lovers who waited for a bus.
Another truck was beeping backward
so I could empty its difficult contents.
Silver studs pierced the two teens' faces
where dimples or glamour moles would've been,
and they stood stomach to stomach, in front
of the wheel shop's pile of tires, listening
to the same song on shared earphones.
The truck driver shouted at me;
he had pages of drop-offs to complete.
I could've pointed to the lovers, told
the driver how they'd eluded school
because their veins ached whenever
their embrace broke, because that day,
although an iron-flavored wind charged
off the East River, the air to the pair felt
like carnation flesh. Of course I said nothing.
I pivoted and began lifting stacked crates,
my back turned when a bus must've admitted
the couple, bound for another corner
dour or numb enough to ignore them.

FIRST WARM MORNING, AMSTERDAM AVENUE

Women walk in lenient skirts,
their toenails like rows of rubies.
On the sidewalk outside the market,
a spry deliveryman stacks boxes
of blueberries, carrots complete
with green manes, and bananas
like little tied-together canoes.
A dog's nose and tongue are overcome
by all the smells returned from furlough.
The avenue's ash trees speak
in the tender tones of our mothers
waking us from troublesome sleep.
The river three blocks west sends
breezes, and a bus driver almost
grins while guiding the wide wheel.

MOLLIFIED

I'm mollified, considering how the daylight
enters the alley and so slowly
intensifies, and then so slowly lessens
upon the buildings' varying bricks.
I'm mollified, as the dairy truck rumbles past,
the stark magnificence of cold milk
brought miles to those in want of cold milk.
Mollified when glancing into a window,
seeing the finely dressed mannequins
more elegant in their headlessness.
And at the street's October aspens,
the tiny leaves in the traffic's wind
falling like flakes of gold paint.
I've probably hurried this city too often,
my brain tangling the particulars
of some complication or pain.
Hence, these recent moments are leaving me
mollified, with no use for scrutiny
or manipulation, with only widened
eyes and a parted mouth to regard
each plentiful simplicity.

PROJECT COURTYARD

A newly adult couple fights
about the man's phone, the messages
another woman keeps sending it.
The sky is dividing its last rations
of light among the public-funded
towers. The couple curses toe to toe.
Some boys in the developing dark
control their ball and watch; a girl
in a scuffed skirt halts too. The woman
fires the phone against the pavement
into fragments. It takes three of the man's
friends to pull him back from attacking,
and the woman lands a loud slap
on his forehead. A police cruiser jerks
to stillness at the curb. From worn doors,
two officers emerge, their belts
rife with devices that ensure
a quicker route to the last word.

HARSHMAN PAINTING

for Paul

They start when the sun is a lemon drop
on the tongue of morning's yawning mouth.
Their boots beat low, echoing notes
on aluminum rungs while they climb
to peaks, to dormers that rain and wind
have rubbed dim. Drop cloths—like fallen,
vandalized banners—cover the bushes, blacktop,
and patio. They shed their shirts near noon
and a housewife, who has wiped her jugulars
with lavender, brings them sweet tea and lets
her eyes tarry on their arms and backs.
Under gutters, they spray bees' nests
with foam and knock the poisoned combs
to the ground with the butts of brushes.
Once the job is done, all the tools return
to racks and hooks in the truck, then the men
clean with pumice and damp rags, they share
a haggard laugh, and they drive slowly back
to lives that at first will flinch from their touch.

LONGING FOR BEFORE

I'm drinking at this place with a stuffed fox
mounted behind the bar, the beer on special
tasting like licks of cold brass.
My bigmouthed heart calls for a shooter
of tan tequila, to quicken my journey
toward bitterness or sentimentality.
Since the evening's last light has dissolved, lively pairs
and groups crowd nearer, and I'm longing for before,
when I could stretch my arms in any direction
and touch no one, when my wife and child
at home had yet to notice my deepening
absence, when the juke still played songs that explained
my central dilemmas, and when I didn't look
into a mirror footed by spouted fifths
and think how, of all things, I miss my loneliness.

PART FOUR

PITIFUL PRINCE

Though my father, uncles, cousins, and cohort
kept simultaneous romances whirling,
I had not the skill or the want to woo
concurrent lovers. Shy and compulsive, I'd
dwell for months on how a certain woman's
shoulders had glowed, had fringed the exquisite
cliff of her collarbone. My brain formed without
the dominant lobe that allows a ladies' man
to plot, to blueprint escape routes, to back
his darlings calmly into corners.
My affairs were outright and undisguised; my eyes
near my dearest were day-struck poppies.
Born in a kingdom of marvelous heartbreakers,
I was the pitiful prince, rambling eternally
of my beloved's singularity.

EDENLESS US

We met during a stretch when
my soul had been smoldering, my
mind not much more than a cistern
of ruinous miscalculations.
In the overcast tavern, she
introduced herself, saying
"Ever feel like you could eat
the whole damn night in one bite?"
Dawn soon careened between buildings,
finding her post-transcendentalist face.
The real estate agent assured us
the head-to-foot fracture
in the foundation should be
no worrisome detail as we sat
back in his merciless Mercedes.
The cries and cachinnation of our
nine children dismantled our sleep
and intensified our dreams.
150 years prior, the two of us
would've been born slaves—
she, at best, forced to wet nurse
the sour offspring of the big house,
and I, at best, leaping between
English and Spanish to entrap
some buttoned-up widow
for my dastardly master.
How magnificently tipsy
my beloved and I walk these
fresh-millennium streets.
Somehow, we're still blithe
enough to get arrested

for naked gyration in the public park.
"I'm ecstatic there's no Eden
or heaven or resurrection,"
she mouths to me through
the windows of the separate
cop cars in which we're cuffed.

STAYING IN

Temperate tequila poured
in Solo cups, we perched
on her bed, stout snow
forcing the Uptown traffic

past the window into tangles.
*To this city finally
having to take its time,*
she toasted, and we tipped

the spirits into our throats.
An entire night in a warm room
with her, whose face and voice
adjusted me like the wind

unflattening matted grass.
Downfall didn't stifle
the power lines, drifts didn't
pile taller than doors, yet

the bottle in front of the candle
could've been a lantern,
the way the glass framed
each flinch and swell of the flame.

THEY'D RATHER GO BLIND

We stopped at that tavern on Second Ave.
where silent men stare into their liquor,
where the jukebox sips quarters and affords
love songs dressed in dust. We danced gradually
on the pine-planked floor, a young Etta's voice
plowing new furrows in our nerves. The curves
between my love's lowest ribs and her hips were
the glens where the nomads of my hands slept.
No wry eyes veered our way that night, wanting
blindness over a glimpse of our bare bliss.

DAYBREAK

In my work coat, I stood at our bed;
she slept, as the dark diffused.
Outside, upper Broadway bore
its concert of hurried motors
and the whir of contractors' tools.
The sun kept sending a few
wavelengths millions of miles—
past asteroids and space dust,
through thermosphere, argon,
and hazy apartment panes—
to fall on much of my love's face.
I leaned and kissed the kinky roots
at her hairline before closing
the door, before entering a city
where women and men gazed
away from one another,
where underground trains drilled
block by block into the dense day.

RING BUYING

Into the calculator, the jeweler
entered the gem's weight, along with the cost
per tenth of a karat, and he broke me
the result gently, like a good doctor.
Outside the store, West Forty-Seventh Street
swarmed, buyers and sellers quibbling stones
or metals alleged to prove and patch love.
I wore a dirty shirt, my forearms sore
from a job lugging furniture up steep flights.
Shaking my hand, the jeweler—his beard prim
and his jaw firm—looked far into my eyes
and held the stare, knowing I needed
sympathy's iodine to neutralize
the wound my wallet had just become.

CONNUBIAL

We got married in a borrowed garden
during autumn, the metallic Atlantic
chewing on the ocher shore. Her mother
fashioned the broom we jumped, my aunt brought
the flowers and the wine, and our friend stood
all night behind turntables, keeping
the improvised dance floor a lively hive.
I thought I knew much of love's terminology
until I donned formal black, until I walked
the grassy lane between people who had raised
or saved me, until I waited with a page
of promises to read to a woman who,
in her veil and drifting dress, moved
like the longest word in some language made
from different angles of silencing light.

HOMAGE TO MY WIFE'S HIPS

In the presence of her hips, thin
White women lower their heads
like children who've broken a dish.
Her hips make dawn on an ocean
seem slight. Her hips are the twin
coasts of the most important continent.
Her hips share genes with the hips
of American slaves, and her hips know
the divinity of being obeyed.
Many nights, I listen to her hips,
my bare ear against their bare flesh;
the spell stuns so much
I forget if it's me or the world
her hips spin unendingly.

HER HAIR

Beginning with scissors
at the inseams, I help take
apart my wife's weave.
The threads release easily,
unbinding the straight mane
of another woman, who cut it
herself in the courtyard
of a Hindu temple, the temple then
selling it to a dealer that exports
to Black American salons.
Into the trash go the removed
strands my wife wore for six weeks,
twirled with rollers and wrapped
evenings, shielded from every hint
of humidity, every inkling of rain.
Beneath the sewn-in sections
have waited these long
scalp-tight braids, winding
to an end above her nape.
I loosen the exposed plaits, I grease
and comb the complicated
tangles, and I think I hear each hair
singing some kind of refrain
that does to the mind what
the mid-sky moon does to the night.

SUBURBAN NOCTURNE

The leftover pie slice, grinning
within the fridge. The lush hush
spreading now that the little ones
drowse so soundly. The wine, stirring
wandlessly in our goblets. The crash
and whoosh of the washer. The silenced
mouth of the finished-off
car note, the darkness of the garage.
The kitchen tile in moonlight
like the scales of an idle reptile.
The secret that the heat vent keeps
repeating. And the mattress,
gracious as shadowed grass
beneath the burden of our fond bodies.

SOLIDARITY

Uncertainly, we moved to the suburbs,
and now a community of crows collects daily
in our yard. They walk calmly,
bobbing their heads to a far-back music.
Their wing feathers flash like tuxedo lapels,
and their eyes are obsidian dimes.
A frank, triple-beat small talk
and survivors' laughter escape
the halved, dark daggers of their beaks.
Leaving for work, my wife pauses, looks
out the window at all the crows, and says
she's glad we still live among other black folks.

DARK-EYED HEIR

We're watching living Europeans dramatize
the lives of dead, aestheticized Europeans,
grabbing a Monday matinée near the center

of an American city in which our
significantly negro son is learning
the paradoxes of sharing before lying

for a nap on an assigned cot at day care.
The movie spans many foggy heaths
and bleak castle expanses that look like

no black folks have ever or will ever
pass through, so my wife and I, sipping
whiskey from a flask, watch cautiously

in the empty film house, somehow feeling
all the cinematic and cultural whiteness might
advance from the screen across the dark

ceiling and walls and swallow us.
Our wariness dissolves, and boredom forms,
so we walk out—the avenue's urgent

motion and sound renewing us—and we head
for a pub with a colorful jukebox that holds
plenty of Donny Hathaway, a man

whose mind, like Macbeth's, was full of scorpions,
a man who, unlike Macbeth, made music
sure to stir my wife and me, until we must

gather ourselves, pay for our frank drinks, take
a full bus, and retrieve our son, dark-eyed heir to all
the streets and songs this kingless land sustains.

FOR TONIGHT

My wife has advanced asthma, and I listen
sometimes to her breathing while she sleeps.
The delicate difficulty, the raspy
series of notes her lungs strum:
a stone comb pulling through the grasses
of oxygen; sand being scattered
by a wind the sea only brings
during darkness. One night, both our bodies
will be completely airless, our stories
no more than wisps of dust, our bones
simply twigs in earth's fist.
For tonight, at least, I'll be led again
through my love's complex breaths into dreams
full of beauty and absurdity, full of all
I'll forget or disbelieve by dawn.

ACKNOWLEDGMENTS

My gratitude goes to the editors and staff of the following anthologies, publications, and websites, where some of this collection's poems originally appeared:

The American Poetry Review: "The Former Us," "Paradise Skate," "Pardon My Heart," and "Travel Plans"

Canteen: "Staying In" and "They'd Rather Go Blind"

Dossier Journal: "Baby Boy in the Back Room," "Dominion of Men," and "Sweetest Day"

The Fiddleback: "Harshman Painting"

Glass: A Journal of Poetry: "Crack Cook" and "Woman in Secret"

Muzzle Magazine: "Lullaby"

The New Yorker: "First Warm Morning, Amsterdam Avenue"

A Poetry Congeries: "Armor" and "Off Camera"

Reverie: "Alternate Take on Autumn Beginning" and "One More Tiny Thing, 1985"

Rockhurst Review: "Convalescence," "Full-Time Driver," and "Project Courtyard"

Rove: "Daybreak"

Southern Humanities Review: "To the Love Gods"

Tin House: "Ashtray," "Evasive Me," and "Goodale Park"